In the Name of Al

MW01049586

فَاذْكُرُونِي أَذْكُرْكُمْ

Remember Me
and
I Will Remember You

by Safi Khan
and Samira Hingoro

Published by:
FAITH Publications
5301 Edgewood Road, College Park, MD 20740, USA
Tel: 1-866-FAITH12, Fax 301-982-9849
E-mail: info@faithpublications.org
Website: www.faithpublications.org

Copyright © 2004 by Safi Khan & Samira Hingoro
Cover Design: Asma Shafi
Typesetting: Sakina Productions

ISBN 0-974316-72-5

For sales and distribution contact: 1-866-FAITH12 or visit us at www.faithpublications.org.

Publisher's Forward

All praises are due to Allah alone.

It is with great honor that the Foundation for Authentic Islamic Texts & Heritage (FAITH) embarks upon the noble mission of creatively producing and disseminating a wealth of authentic Islamic books and multimedia resources. It is our firm belief that having such authentic knowledge running through the minds of our dear readers will ultimately fortify the veins of a much needed strong, united and vibrant Muslim community.

FAITH is another educational project of Dar-us-Salaam. The name "Dar-us-Salaam" means an abode or community of peace and is one of the names of Paradise. We sincerely hope and earnestly pray that this Dar-us-Salaam will be the stepping stone for all people to the real Dar-us-Salaam (i.e. Paradise). Currently this community of Dar-us-Salaam, located in College Park, Maryland, consists of a full-time Islamic School, as well as several other spiritual, educational and business projects, all operating on the teachings of the Qur'an and Sunnah. In short this Dar-us-Salaam calls as "Allah calls (all) to Dar-us-Salaam,"[1] to establish a practical model Muslim community, which encompasses Islam in its totality.

i

Special thanks to Sheikh Moataz Al-Hallak for reviewing the book and providing valuable advice. We would also like to extend our thanks to Zahirah Abdul-Wakil, Haroon Baqai, Mona Ghounem, Minhaj Hasan and Sajeela Yaqub who helped to make this book possible.

Your suggestions and comments are welcomed. To learn more about FAITH, visit www.faithpublications.org.

May Allah accept all of our efforts.

Contents

عَنْ عَبْدِ الله بْنِ بُسْرٍ رَضِيَ اللهُ عَنْهُ قَالَ: أَتَى النَّبِيَّ صَلَّى
اللهُ عَلَيْهِ وَسَلَّمَ رَجُلٌ، فَقَالَ: يَا رَسُولَ الله إِنَّ شَرَائِعَ
الْإِسْلَام قَدْ كَثُرَتْ عَلَيْنَا، فَبَابٌ نَتَمَسَّكُ بِهِ جَامِعٌ قَالَ:
لَا يَزَالُ لِسَانُكَ رَطْبًا مِنْ ذِكْرِ الله عَزَّ وَجَلَّ [احمد]

Abdullah ibn Busr *radiyallahu 'anhu*[2]
narrated that "A man came to the
Prophet *sallallaahu 'alayhi wa sallam*[3]
and said, 'Oh Prophet of Allah, the
laws of Islam have become too much
for us. So, is there one thing that we
can hold on to that would be inclu-
sive (of many other things)?' He
sallallaahu 'alayhi wa sallam replied,
'Keep your tongue moist with the remembrance of Allah, most Exalted,
Sublime.'"[4]

1

Preface

In the hustle and bustle of everyday life how often do you feel bad, not able to remember Allah *subhaanahu wa ta'ala*[5] during the day? Our minds are easily diverted from one thing to another. At times, after much effort to focus on Allah *subhaanahu wa ta'ala*, we find ourselves actually reflecting. But, sadly, within a minute those fragile moments of contemplation are shattered by one or another stray thought and everything is lost. Ironically, in most cases, those intruding thoughts last no longer than a few minutes and chances are high that we will forget them as quickly as they came.

We find ourselves constantly thinking about everything *but* Allah. When we do think about Him, Shaytan whispers other things to our mind. "Oh, I forgot to do the laundry!" or "Wow, look at that car!" or "That's a nice dress she's wearing …" regularly distract our minds from focusing our thoughts on Allah *subhaanahu wa ta'ala*. Usu-

3

ally, such nagging thoughts have little impact in our lives. At the end of the day, our hearts have wandered far away from Allah *subhaanahu wa ta'ala*, not realizing that they have traded something precious for something paltry.

Often we listen to motivating talks. Inevitably we ask ourselves, "Why can't I change myself?" or "What did I do today to make Allah *subhaanahu wa ta'ala* happy?" Normally, we justify our apathy by the pet excuse, "Life is so hectic and I'm so busy. I just don't get a chance to do my ibadaah[5] or to remember Allah *subhaanahu wa ta'ala* beside the five prayers."

One of the great differences between us and the righteous people of the past is that they were able to focus on remembering Allah *subhaanahu wa ta'ala* throughout the day despite their busy schedules. They were acutely aware that their unrelenting remembrance of Allah *subhaanahu wa ta'ala* had an extraordinary impact on their lives, their character and the people around them. These days we may consider ourselves highly successful if we are able to focus even a few minutes on Allah *subhaanahu wa ta'ala*. Before we know it, the crafty Shaytan shatters our inner peace with pesky thoughts, "I better go and eat something," or we think, "… I'm really hungry." We wonder, "Let me see, did someone email me today?" How terrifying it is to think that day after day we live our lives in vain, chasing the world. Swept away by worldly thoughts, devoid of Allah's *subhaanahu wa ta'ala* remembrance, our entire life passes without our hearts changing in the least.

So what can you do to bring that change in your life? The key word is *focus*. Reflect on the hadeeth mentioned in the beginning of the book when the man came and complained to the Prophet *sallallaahu 'alayhi wa sallam* that "...the laws of Islam have become too much ...." What did the Prophet *sallallaahu 'alayhi wa sallam* tell him? He *sallallaahu 'alayhi wa sallam* didn't get upset at him or say, "How dare you say that? You're going to hell!" No! Instead he *sallallaahu 'alayhi wa sallam* said, "...keep your tongue moist with the remembrance of Allah, most Exalted, Sublime." The Prophet *sallallaahu 'alayhi wa sallam* used real human psychology. Through Allah *subhaanahu wa ta'ala*, he *sallallaahu 'alayhi wa sallam* was keenly aware of the human psyche. In other words, the only thing you have to do is to say "Alhumdulillah" in gratitude to Allah *subhaanahu wa ta'ala* for all of the divine grace in your life (i.e, all the good things of life you enjoy).

Once we begin to repeat this a few times, we will begin to reflect on what is being uttered. For instance, when we enter or exit our homes, we should discipline ourselves to say the various ad'eeyah[7] the Prophet *sallallaahu 'alayhi wa sallam* taught us. Eventually, we will think about what is being said. When we sit in a car or any other mode of transportation, we should remember Allah *subhaanahu wa ta'ala* with a du'a.[8] More importantly, we must *also* begin to think about the *meaning* of that du'a. For every aspect of life, the Prophet *sallallaahu 'alayhi wa sallam* left ad'eeyah for us to say. If we memorize and implement them, our tongues will be moist with the remembrance of Allah *subhaanahu wa ta'ala*. A certain peace and contentment will pervade our hearts. Gradually, we will see a change in ourselves. Moreover, our families, friends and the people around us will sense that change for the better.

These days, books containing the authentic supplications of the Prophet *salallaahu 'alayhi wa sallam* exist in all shapes, sizes, colors and in almost every language. Most of us carry them in our purses or pockets. Our bookshelves are blessed with their decorative value. The crucial question is how many of us actually take the time to learn these supplications and then remember to say them at appropriate times? Very few. Already plagued with the horrific stresses of daily life, our stress levels hit their peak when we painfully realize that we are not doing much to increase our bond with Allah *subhaanahu wa ta'ala*. Shaytan knows how to conquer us. If the world seems important to us, he will keep us busy with it. If he knows that we know it's not that important then he will still keep us busy in procrastinating. Finally, if remorse sets in, he whispers to us, "You are a worthless nobody. You are never going to change!" Subsequently, many of us find ourselves depressed and leading miserable lives. Sadly, we are unwilling to get up and actually do something about it or even to simply acknowledge our weaknesses.

If you find yourself being described above, then don't let Shaytan make you think that you are too busy. You can still have time to remember Allah *subhaanahu wa ta'ala*. In an attempt to help you bond with Allah *subhaanahu wa ta'ala*, this simple book will make mundane everyday chores exciting insha'Allah[9]. With the daily remembrance of Allah *subhaanahu wa ta'ala* you will soar spiritually faster than you can imagine.

So stop worrying and look forward to each fresh day with the remembrance of Allah *subhaanahu wa ta'ala*.

How to Use this Book

This booklet is an anthology of a few short and simple ad'eeyah and adhkaar[10] that the Prophet *sallallaahu 'alayhi wa sallam* taught us. They are all narrated in authentic Ahadeeth[11] literature. These adhkaar are designed to be recited throughout the day. To help you get started, we have associated them with routine activities.

Our intent is to help you increase your remembrance of Allah *subhaanahu wa ta' ala*. But, it is important that you don't limit these adkhaar only to the suggested activities mentioned. Whenever you can, alternate them with various activities and increase them. You may want to use additional ad'eeyah from authentic sources and slowly add them to your current daily regimen of ad'eeyah as you become disciplined in using them.

Lastly, don't forget to keep us in your du'as!

Remember
Allah

Let's Walk

Here are a few things you can do to remember Allah *subhaanahu wa ta' ala* when you are walking. You may be walking in a school or in an office hallway, going from one office to another or from one class to another, going for a jog or going on a stroll with your child. Make a conscious effort to use that time to remember Allah. If you live in an apartment building with stairs, you can go up and down the stairs each day in remembrance of Allah *subhaanahu wa ta' ala*. It will be a good exercise and it will be a breeze because your mind will be with Allah *subhaanahu wa ta'ala*.

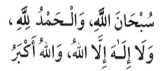

سُبْحَانَ اللَّهِ، وَالْـحَمْدُ لِلَّهِ،
وَلَا إِلَـهَ إِلَّا اللهُ، وَاللهُ أَكْبَرُ

Glory be to Allah, and all praise and thanks be to Allah, and there is no one who deserves to be worshipped except Allah, and Allah is the greatest.

11

أَحَبُّ الْكَلَامِ إِلَى اللهِ أَرْبَعٌ: سُبْحَانَ اللهِ، وَالْحَمْدُ لِلَّهِ،
وَلَا إِلَهَ إِلَّا اللهُ، وَاللهُ أَكْبَرُ. لَا يَضُرُّكَ بِأَيِّهِنَّ بَدَأْتَ (مسلم)

There are four statements which are most beloved to Allah:

- Glory be to Allah.
- And all praise and thanks be to Allah.
- And there is no one who deserves to be worshipped except Allah.
- And Allah is the greatest.[12]

It doesn't matter which one you begin with.

You can say all these four statements together as mentioned in the Hadeeth or individually, as often as you want and as much as you want. There is no limit to it.

If you already know other verses from the Qur'an or ahadeeth you can also use them while doing any form of exercise. Or you can say any supplication that you have memorized from the Qur'an or from the authentic ahadeeth.

Have you ever thought about all the blessings that Allah has bestowed on you? While you are walking, feel the breeze on your face and think about how Allah has made it easy for you to walk comfortably in it. Look at the plants, trees, sky and how Allah has painted them in various colors for you to enjoy.

Have you ever wondered how you could gain one thousand good deeds? How you can have your bad deeds erased? What if you could erase one thousand of them at a time? How about if it took you less than few minutes to do it? If the above mentioned four phrases are too much for you to say, than at least try to say the following simple phrase to cash in all the rewards:

سُبْحَانَ الله

Glory be to Allah.

عَنْ سَعْدِ بْنِ أَبِي وَقَّاصٍ رَضِيَ اللهُ عَنْهُ قَالَ كُنَّا عِنْدَ
رَسُولِ الله صَلَّى اللهُ عَلَيْهِ وَسَلَّمَ فَقَالَ أَيَعْجِزُ أَحَدُكُمْ أَنْ
يَكْسِبَ فِي كُلِّ يَوْمٍ أَلْفَ حَسَنَةٍ فَسَأَلَهُ سَائِلٌ مِنْ جُلَسَائِهِ
كَيْفَ يَكْسِبُ أَلْفَ حَسَنَةٍ قَالَ يُسَبِّحُ مِائَةَ تَسْبِيحَةٍ
فَيُكْتَبُ لَهُ أَلْفُ حَسَنَةٍ أَوْ يُحَطُّ عَنْهُ أَلْفُ خَطِيئَةٍ (مسلم)

Sa'd ibn Abee Waqqaas *radiyallahu 'anhu* narrated that, "We were with

13

the Prophet *sallallaahu 'alayhi wa sallam* and he asked us, 'Is one of you incapable of earning a thousand good deeds every day?' So one of the people in the audience asked, 'How could we get a thousand good deeds?' So he *sallallaahu 'alayhi wa sallam* said, 'Whoever glorifies Allah one hundred times, a thousand good deeds are written for him or a thousand of his bad deeds are removed.'"[13]

Doesn't Allah *subhaanahu wa ta'ala* truly deserve to have all the glory? So praise Allah with all of your heart.

Remember
Allah

Knock on the
Door of Allah

All of us sin day and night. Often, we have no compunction or even realize we did something wrong. It is important for us to take a daily account of ourselves. We must remember to ask Allah's forgiveness for everything we may have done to displease Him and must resolve never to do it again. So let's try to knock on the door of repentance by saying as many times as possible the following easy words:

أَسْتَغْفِرُ اللهَ

I seek forgiveness from Allah.

عَنْ أَبِي هُرَيْرَةَ رَضِيَ اللهُ عَنْهُ قَالَ سَمِعْتُ رَسُولَ الله
صَلَّى اللهُ عَلَيْهِ وَسَلَّمَ يَقُولُ وَاللهِ إِنِّي لَأَسْتَغْفِرُ اللهَ وَأَتُوبُ
إِلَيْهِ فِي الْيَوْمِ أَكْثَرَ مِنْ سَبْعِينَ مَرَّةً (البخاري)

Abu Hurayrah *radiyallahu 'anhu* narrated that "I heard the Prophet
sallallaahu 'alayhi wa sallam say, 'I
swear by Allah that I seek Allah's forgiveness and repent to Him more than
seventy times daily.'"[14]

Think about all the things you do that Allah
subhaanahu wa ta'ala may not be pleased with. You
may have had a fight with your spouse or talked
back to your parents or driven off in a fast fury or
called someone names that they didn't like. What-
ever it is, know that Allah *subhaanahu wa ta'ala* is
capable of forgiving if you seek His forgiveness
with sincere remorse. It will take you less than
five minutes to say it seventy times with feeling.
Reflect upon what you are saying and focus. If
you need to look down in order to concentrate and
avoid distractions, then do so.

Remember
Allah

Drive with Allah

The car or any mode of transportation provides you with a golden opportunity to spend some time with Allah *subhaanahu wa ta'ala*. Tune out the noise. Take time out from the cell phone.

Hooked to the radio? Don't touch that knob. Many of us feel the need to find out what is happening in the world. Chances are that if we turn on the radio for the news, weather or traffic, we will end up waiting for it. Meanwhile, our ears will be bombarded with lewd commercials and Islamophobic commentary we are better off not hearing. If you must know the news and the traffic for the commute, then turn on the radio at the time of the news and traffic report only. Don't waste your time listening to anything that will not help you to draw closer to Paradise.

Instead, make the long rush hour commutes to work, school or home a "joy ride" by doing one of the following things:

1. Play a tape of the Qur'an and memorize at least two ayaat.[15] Over time you may even find it easy to increase the number of verses you memorize.

2. Memorize some of the ad'eeyah from the books that might be collecting dust in your pocket, purse or glove compartment.

3. Listen to an inspiring Islamic lecture tape or a CD.

4. Contemplate on the creation of Allah while repeating various adhkaar.

5. If you are a student of Arabic, listen to lectures in Arabic and reinforce or improve your understanding of the language.

The next time you are stuck in a traffic jam, consider it a blessing in disguise. Don't get frustrated. Just relax and use one of these tips to connect with Allah. Remember to never drive alone. Drive with Allah.[16]

Remember
Allah

Spice Up Your Life

Whether you work outside of the home or are busy at home caring for your family, most women end up being in the kitchen on a daily basis. We often spice up our kitchen life up by talking on the phone with friends while cooking. But cooking time could be more fruitful and spiritually delicious if you use one of the following tips:

1. Listen to the Qur'an while cooking. If you don't understand Arabic, get the tapes or CDs with translation.

2. While listening to the Qur'an, memorize two ayaat every time you work in the kitchen. Don't forget to also review previously memorized verses.

3. Listen to motivating lectures on Islamic history.

4. Place authentic supplications of the Prophet *sallallaahu 'alayhi wa sallam* on the refrigerator and try to memorize them.

5. You can also say the following adhkaar along with one of the previously mentioned adhkaar.

$$سُبْحَانَ اللهِ وَبِحَمْدِهِ$$

*Glory be to Allah and
all praise be to Him.*

Can you imagine what the reward of these few words is if you say them with feeling a hundred times?

عَنْ أَبِي هُرَيْرَةَ رَضِيَ اللهُ عَنْهُ أَنَّ رَسُولَ اللهِ صَلَّى اللهُ عَلَيْهِ
وَسَلَّم قَالَ: مَنْ قَالَ: سُبْحَانَ اللهِ وَبِحَمْدِهِ فِي يَوْمٍ مِائَةَ
مَرَّةٍ، حُطَّتْ خَطَايَاهُ وَإِنْ كَانَتْ مِثْلَ زَبَدِ الْبَحْرِ (البخاري)

Abu Hurayrah *radiyallahu 'anhu* narrated that "The Prophet *sallallaahu 'alayhi wa sallam* said, 'Whoever says 'Glory be to Allah and all praise be to Him' in a day a hundred times his sins will be forgiven even if they are like the foam on the sea'[17]."[18]

How long might it take for you to say these simple yet beautiful words? Chances are not more than five minutes. What a wonderful way to cook and have your sins forgiven, too. It's a double treat.

You are getting rewarded for taking care of your family and having your sins removed at the same time. Subhaanallah![19] Allah *subhaanahu wa ta'ala* is so merciful. He gives so much in return for just a little effort.

Remember
Allah

Learn How to Wait

Do you find yourself waiting around a lot? Waiting for someone at a metro station, in a school, perhaps in a line at a grocery store or even waiting for a web page to load while surfing the internet? Instead of concocting a planned response to the frustration, chill out and say any one of the following adhkaar to pass the time. Every moment of your life is passing quickly. Don't let a single moment pass without doing something good!

You can always have enough time to say:

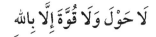

لَا حَوْلَ وَلَا قُوَّةَ إِلَّا بِاللَّه

There is no power, no movement
except through/by Allah.

عَنْ أَبِي مُوسَى الْأَشْعَرِيِّ رَضِيَ اللهُ عَنْهُ قَالَ قَالَ لِي
رَسُولُ اللهِ صَلَّى اللهُ عَلَيْهِ وَسَلَّمَ: أَلَا أَدُلُّكَ عَلَى كَنْزٍ
مِنْ كُنُوزِالْـجَنَّةِ؟ فَقُلْتُ: بَلَى يَا رَسُولَ اللهِ، قَالَ: لَا
حَوْلَ وَلَا قُوَّةَ إِلَّا بِاللهِ (البخاري)

Abu Moosa Al Ash'ari *radiyallahu 'anhu* narrated that "The Prophet *sallallaahu 'alayhi wa sallam* asked me, 'Shouldn't I show you a treasure from the treasures of Paradise?' I said, 'Sure! Oh Prophet of Allah.' He *sallallaahu 'alayhi wa sallam* said, 'There is no power, no movement except through/by Allah.'"[20]

Often you find yourself helpless when you have to wait. So know that there is no power, no movement except by Allah. He is the one who is going to give you the strength to do the right thing. He will help you to be patient and control your response. Say this dhikr as much as possible.

Besides, who doesn't want to possess one of the treasures of Paradise? It sure beats focusing on thoughts that are not bringing us any closer to Paradise!

Remember
Allah

One Moment Please ...

Do you ever find yourself holding on the phone for ages when calling customer service at some large company? Tune out the music. You can use this opportunity to reflect. Contemplate. Try any of the previously mentioned tips or simply say:

سُبْحَانَ اللهِ وَبِحَمْدِهِ، سُبْحَانَ اللهِ الْعَظِيمِ

Glory be to Allah and all praise be to Him, (and) Glory be to Allah the Great.

عَنْ أَبِي هُرَيْرَةَ رَضِيَ اللهُ عَنْهُ عَنِ النَّبِيِّ صَلَّى اللهُ عَلَيْهِ

وَسَلَّمَ قَالَ: كَلِمَتَانِ خَفِيفَتَانِ عَلَى اللِّسَانِ، ثَقِيلَتَانِ

فِي الْمِيزَانِ، حَبِيبَتَانِ إِلَى الرَّحْمَٰنِ: سُبْحَانَ اللهِ وَبِحَمْدِهِ

سُبْحَانَ اللهِ الْعَظِيمِ (البخاري)

Abu Hurayrah *radiyallahu 'anhu* narrated that "The Prophet *sallallaahu
'alayhi wa sallam* said, 'There are two
statements which are light on the
tongue, heavy in the balance[21] and beloved to the most Merciful; they are –
Glory be to Allah and all praise be to
Him, (and) Glory be to Allah the
Great.'"[22]

If you have the Qur'an handy you can also
review previously memorized verses.

Remember
Allah

Shop 'til You Drop?
Think Again

When we enter the mall, most of us marvel at the new inventions and stare in desire at the new fashions. While we are there, Shaytan has a field day. Everything is so hypnotizing that we are often not fully conscious of our thoughts and actions. The only time we snap out of it is when we are holding the receipt for our purchases and walking back to our car.

As if he knew our situation, the Prophet *sallallaahu 'alayhi wa sallam* told us to say a du'a before entering the marketplace. That way we can direct our minds to remember Allah *subhaanahu wa ta'ala* instead of listening to Shaytan. Remembering Allah *subhaanahu wa ta'ala* helps us to keep things in perspective as we buy only what we need. It reminds us to save our hard-earned money to donate for Allah's *subhaanahu wa ta'ala* sake or help someone less fortunate than us, rather than spend it frivolously on things that we don't really need. Often we are amazed to find new gadgets. However, that amazement is short lived when we remember that the entire Kingdom belongs to Allah *subhaanahu wa ta'ala*. That is more amazing than any man-made products which are also inspired by Allah *subhaanahu wa ta'ala*. In His hands are all good things and He is capable of everything.

So don't fall into a trance the next time you go shopping. Instead focus and remember Allah *subhaanahu wa ta'ala* no matter where you are. Allah *subhaanahu wa ta'ala* has made it so easy for us. He will forgive our sins if we just stop, focus and remember Him! So let's remember to say the following du'a to enhance our shopping adventure:

لَا إِلَهَ إِلَّا اللهُ وَحْدَهُ لَا شَرِيكَ لَهُ، لَهُ الْـمُلْكُ، وَلَهُ الْـحَمْدُ، يُحْيِي وَيُمِيتُ وَهُوَ حَيٌّ لَّا يَمُوتُ بِيَدِهِ الْـخَيْرُ وَهُوَ عَلَى كُلِّ شَيْءٍ قَدِيرٌ

There is no one who deserves to be worshipped, but Allah alone without partners. To Him belongs the Kingdom and to Him belongs all Praise. He gives life and death and He is alive and does not die. In His hands is all the good and He is capable of everything.

عَنْ عُمَرَ ابْنِ الْخَطَّابِ رَضِيَ اللهُ عَنْهُ عَن رَسُولِ الله صَلَّى اللهُ عَلَيْهِ وَسَلَّمَ قَالَ: مَنْ دَخَلَ السُّوقَ فَقَالَ: لَا إِلَهَ إِلَّا اللهُ وَحْدَهُ لَا شَرِيكَ لَهُ، لَهُ الْمُلْكُ، وَلَهُ الْحَمْدُ، يُحْيِي وَيُمِيتُ وَهُوَ حَيٌّ لَا يَمُوتُ بِيَدِهِ الْخَيْرُ وَهُوَ عَلَى كُلِّ شَيْءٍ قَدِيرٌ. كَتَبَ اللهُ لَهُ أَلْفَ أَلْفَ حَسَنَةٍ، وَمَحَا عَنْهُ أَلْفَ أَلْفَ سَيِّئَةٍ وَرَفَعَ لَهُ أَلْفَ أَلْفَ دَرَجَةٍ (الترمذي)

'Umar ibn Al-Khattaab *radiyallahu 'anhu* narrated that "The Prophet *sallallaahu 'alayhi wa sallam* said, 'Whoever enters the marketplace and says – There is no one who deserves to be worshipped, but Allah alone without partners. To Him belongs the Kingdom and to Him belongs all Praise. He gives life and death. He is alive and does not die. In His hands is all the good and He is capable of everything – Allah will record one million good deeds for him, will erase one million bad deeds for him and will raise him one million degrees higher in Paradise.'"[23]

Subhaanallah, imagine that! Just by remembering to say this du'a before entering a mall, you are credited with a million good deeds while a million bad deeds are removed from your record. And that's not all – you move up a million degrees in Paradise! This is Allah's love and mercy! What a loving God! What a merciful God!

Remember Allah

Don't Be Down, Move Up

Why so glum? Know that Allah *subhaanahu wa ta'ala* loves you and cares about you. Just the fact that you are breathing and your heart is beating is a manifestation of the love and mercy of Allah *subhaanahu wa ta'ala*. Shaytan often whispers in your ears to make you feel sorry for yourself. Remember that Allah *subhaanahu wa ta'ala* never gives up on you, even though Shaytan makes you feel that way. Allah *subhaanahu wa ta'ala* gives you a new lease on life every day the sun rises.

Allah *subhaanahu wa ta'ala* taught His Prophet *sallallaahu 'alayhi wa sallam* to teach us to say the following du'a when we feel sad or depressed:

اللَّهُمَّ إِنِّي أَعُوذُ بِكَ مِنَ الْـهَمِّ وَالْـحَزَنِ وَالْعَجْزِ

وَالْكَسَلِ وَالْـجُبْنِ وَالْبُخْلِ وَضَلَعِ الدَّيْنِ وَغَلَبَةِ

الرِّجَالِ (البخاري)

31

*Oh Allah! I seek Your protection from
any anxiety, sadness, being unable to
do something, laziness, cowardice,
stinginess, over-whelming debt and
the pressure of men.*[24]

Try to say this du'a as often as possible.

The Prophet *sallallaahu 'alayhi wa sallam* en-
couraged us to always be with righteous people.
When you are by yourself, Shaytan has more of an
opportunity to work on you. When you are feeling
down, do not sit alone. Get out of bed. The only
person you are hurting is yourself. Even if you
hide underneath the covers, Allah can still see you.
Self pity and calling life "unfair" is not going to
make you feel better or solve your problems. In
fact, it will only add to them. The Prophet
sallallaahu 'alayhi wa sallam advised us to look at
the people who have less than us. Know that in the
world there may be thousands of people who would
be willing to give up anything to have what you
have. It could be health, wealth or a good family.
So acknowledge His blessings by not feeling sorry
for yourself. Be grateful for what He has given
you!

Instead of hiding away in some corner you
can do one of the following things:

1. Help someone in need.

2. Go to the masjid.

3. Participate in organizing various social and educational programs in the masjid.

Try it. It will actually make a difference in your life and make you feel truly happy. If you are depressed, the most important thing is to try not to be by yourself.

Remember
Allah

Conclusion

Insha'Allah, we hope that you have benefited from these quick tips. We hope and pray that Allah *subhaanahu wa ta'ala* gives you the strength and power to remember Him and get closer to Him.

Remember you can use these tips and adhkaar at anytime. Don't limit them to a particular time.

So, the next time you find yourself begging Allah to help you and you have been neglectful of Him, remember what Allah has said:

فَاذْكُرُونِي أَذْكُرْكُمْ

Remember Me and I will remember you.[25]

End Notes

[1] Qur'an 5:8

[2] May Allah be pleased with him

[3] May Allah's peace and blessings be upon him

[4] Recorded by Ahmed (This Hadeeth is Saheeh, i.e. authentic.)

[5] Allah, He is pure and exalted beyond any error or weakness or shortcoming

[6] Worship

[7] Supplications

[8] Supplication or prayer

[9] If Allah wills

[10] Remembrance of Allah *subhaanahu wa ta'ala*

[11] Ahadeeth (plural of hadeeth) which means a statement or report of Prophet Muhammad *sallallaahu 'alayhi wa sallam*

[12] Recorded by Muslim

[13] Recorded by Muslim

[14] Recorded by Bukhari

[15] Verses of the Qur'an

re the expression "drive with Allah" is based on the
:eth which was recorded by Buhkari, Muslim, at-
idhi and Ibn-Majah – "I am [i.e., Allah] with him
when he remembers Me." This companionship is a special one that implies providing His divine care, support
and help for the person who remembers Allah. There is
a general type of divine companionship which applies
to all that exists. The general companionship means that
Allah *subhaanahu wa ta'ala* is with all his creation in that
He hears them, sees them, and knows all about them.
This clarification is important as it is part of the creed of
every Muslim to believe that Allah *subhaanahu wa ta'ala*
is above the seven heavens and above His throne, i.e.
above all of His creation. Clearly, the fact that Allah is
above His creation does not contradict His companionship in the general sense nor in the special sense.

[17] It means even if the sins are a lot.

[18] Recorded by Bukhari and Muslim

[19] Glory be to Allah

[20] Recorded by Bukhari and Muslim

[21] It means will carry much weight of good deeds on the
balance on the Day of Judgment.

[22] Recorded by Bukhari

[23] Recorded by Tirmidhi (Hadeeth Hasan)

[24] Recorded by Bukhari

[25] Qur'an 2:152

Arabic Transliteration Guide

Let's Walk
page 13 – Subhaanallahi wal hamdulillahi wa la ilaha illallahu wallahu akbar

Knocking on the Door of Allah
page 17 – Astaghfirullah

Spice Up Your Life
page 22 – Subhaanallahi wa bihamdihi

Learn to Wait
page 25 – La hawla wa la Quwwata illa billah

One Moment Please
page 27 – Subhaanallahi wa bihamdihi
Subhaanallahil 'adheem.

‏'til You Drop? Think Again

30 – La ilaaha illallahu wahdahu la
eka lahu lahul-mulku wa lahul-hamdu
yuhyee wa yumeetu wa huwa hayyun la yamootu
biyadihil-khayru wa huwa 'ala kulli shai-in
Qadeer.

Don't Be Down

Page 33 – Allahumma inni a'udhu bika
minalhammi wal hazani wal 'ajzi wal kasali wal
jubni wal bukhli wa dhala'addayni wa ghalabat-
ir-rijaal.

Made in the USA
Middletown, DE
22 July 2024

57381920R00027